This book belongs to:

_ _ _ _ _ _ _ _ _ _ _ _ _ _ _ _ _ _ _ _

MW00453763

www.BarbaraItalianArtist.com

COLORING BOOKS

www.BarbaraItalianArtist.com

NUMBERS COLORING

ANTS & LADYBUGS

1 TO 20

by *Barbara Pelizzoli*

Series ①

Pelizzoli Barbara
Italian Artist
COLORING BOOKS

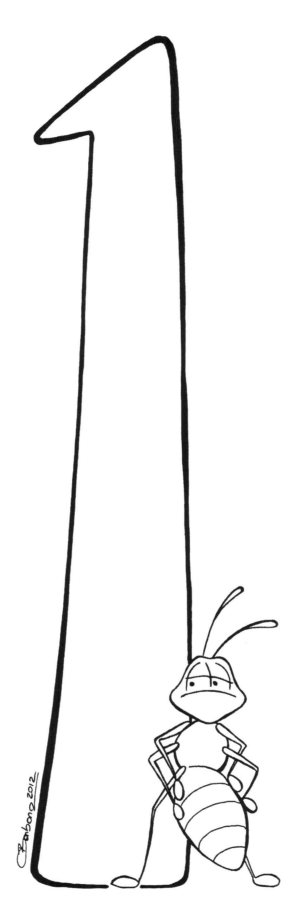

www.BarbaraItalianArtist.com

Pelizzoli Barbara

Italian Artist

COLORING BOOKS

www.BarbaraItalianArtist.com

Pelizzoli **Barbara**
Italian Artist

COLORING BOOKS

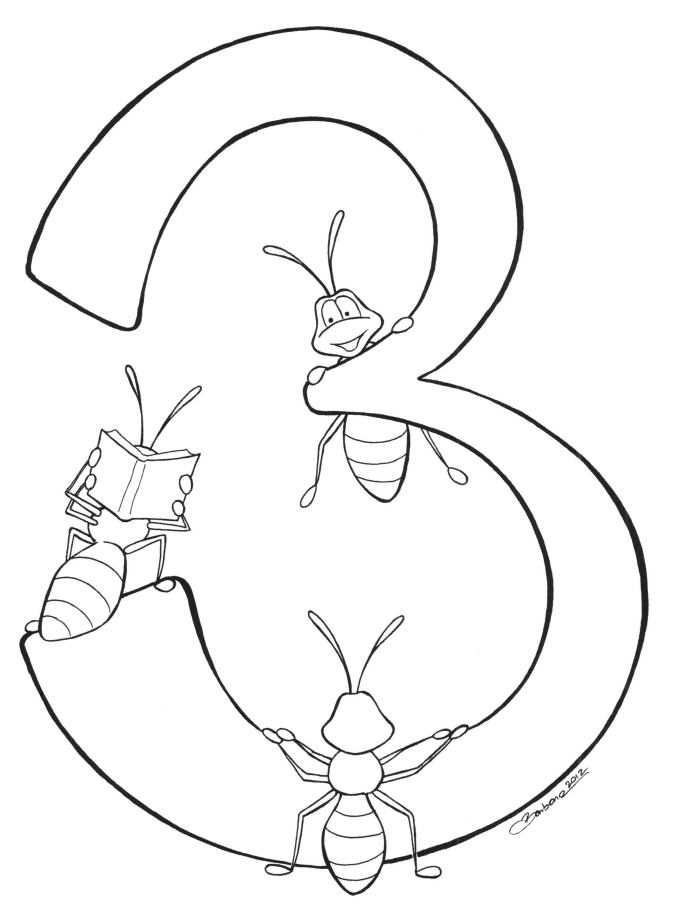

www.BarbaraItalianArtist.com

Pelizzoli Barbara

Italian Artist

COLORING BOOKS

Pelizzoli Barbara
Italian Artist
COLORING BOOKS

Pelizzoli Barbara

Italian Artist

COLORING BOOKS

Pelizzoli Barbara
Italian Artist
COLORING BOOKS

Pelizzoli **Barbara**
Italian Artist
COLORING BOOKS

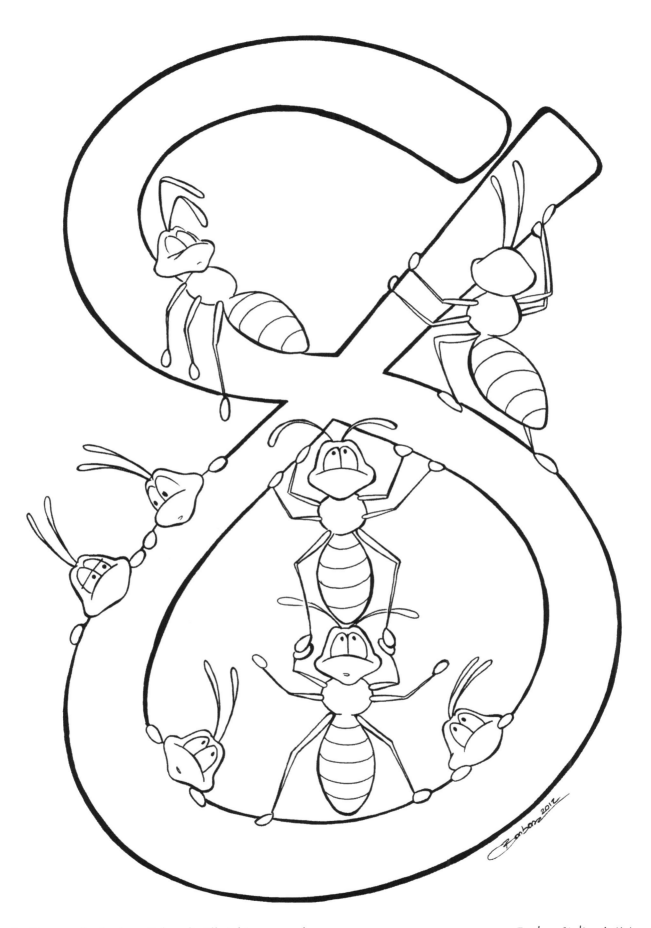

www.BarbaraItalianArtist.com

Barbara Pelizzoli

Italian Artist

COLORING BOOKS

www.BarbaraItalianArtist.com

Pelizzoli **Barbara**
Italian Artist

COLORING BOOKS

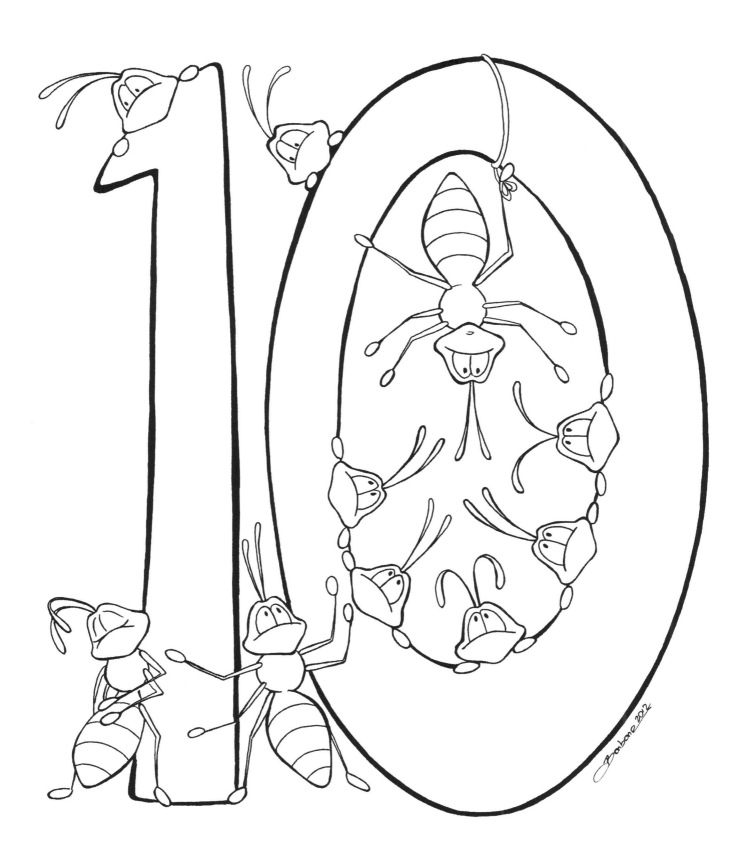

www.BarbaraItalianArtist.com

Pelizzoli **Barbara**
Italian Artist

COLORING BOOKS

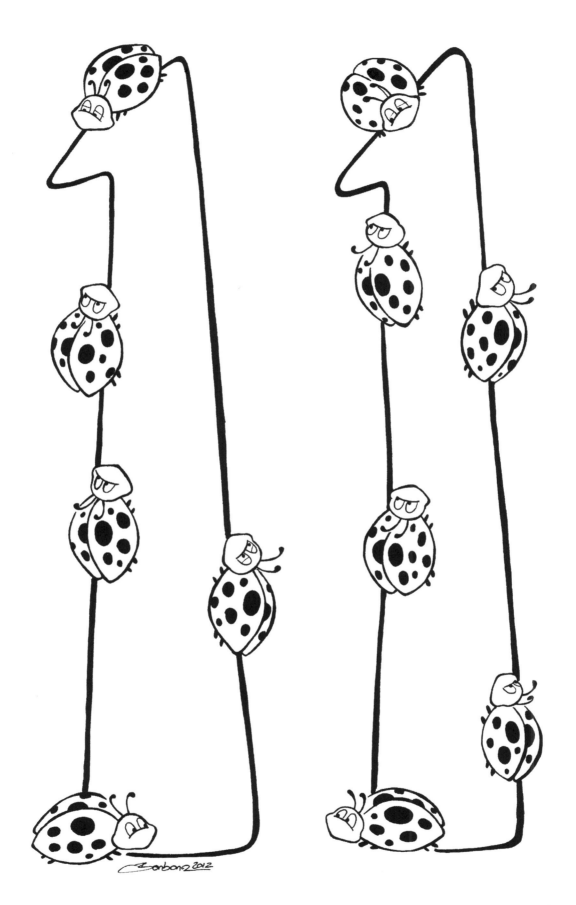

Pelizzoli Barbara
Italian Artist
COLORING BOOKS

Pelizzoli Barbara Italian Artist

COLORING BOOKS

Pelizzoli Barbara
Italian Artist

COLORING BOOKS

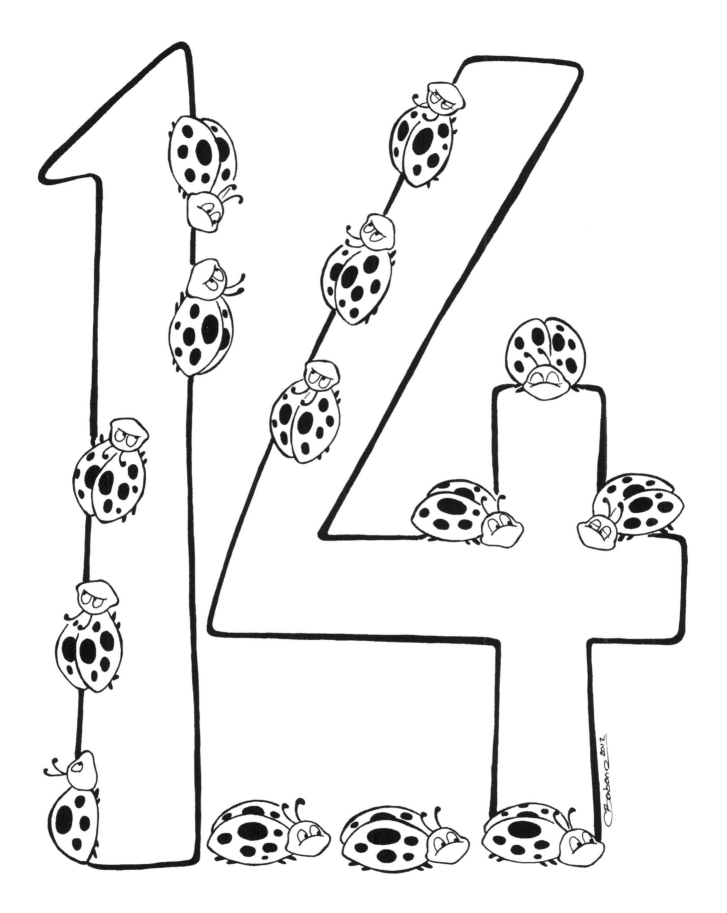

www.BarbaraItalianArtist.com

Pelizzoli Barbara
Italian Artist

COLORING BOOKS

www.BarbaraItalianArtist.com

Pelizzoli Barbara Italian Artist

COLORING BOOKS

www.BarbaraItalianArtist.com

Pelizzoli Barbara
Italian Artist

COLORING BOOKS

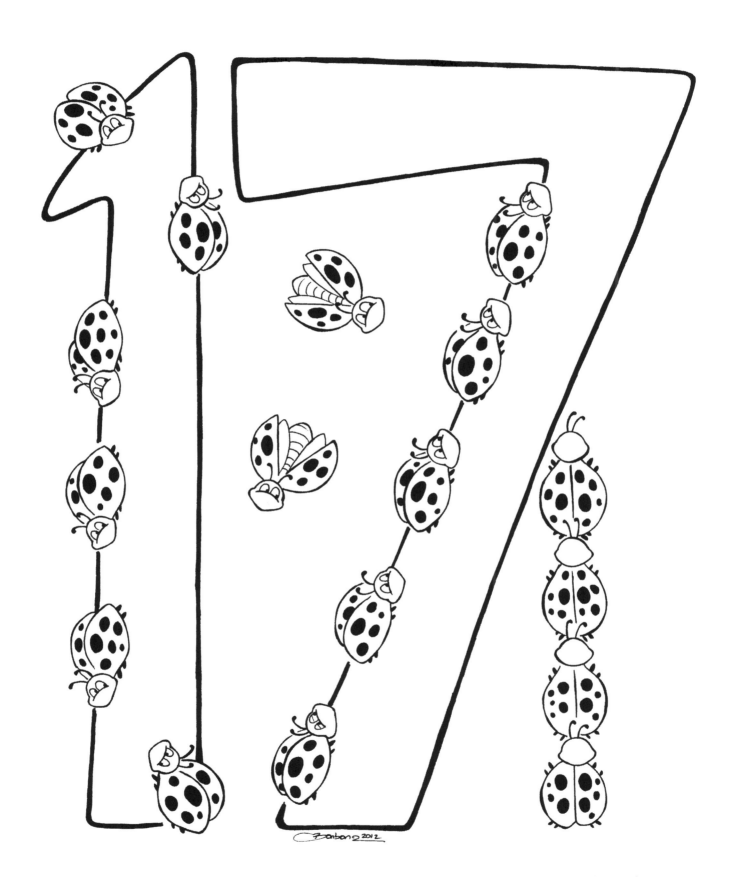

www.BarbaraItalianArtist.com

Pelizzoli Barbara
Italian Artist

COLORING BOOKS

www.BarbaraItalianArtist.com

Pelizzoli Barbara
Italian Artist
COLORING BOOKS

Pelizzoli Barbara
Italian Artist
COLORING BOOKS

Pelizzoli **Barbara**
Italian Artist

COLORING BOOKS

www.BarbaraItalianArtist.com

Pelizzoli Barbara Italian Artist

COLORING BOOKS

Pelizzoli Barbara Italian Artist

COLORING BOOKS

www.BarbaraItalianArtist.com

Pelizzoli Barbara Italian Artist

COLORING BOOKS

www.BarbaraItalianArtist.com

Pelizzoli Barbara
Italian Artist
COLORING BOOKS

For More Books Visit

www.IMAGINEABOOK.com

CHILDREN'S PICTURE BOOKS

Happy Cows Make Good Milk

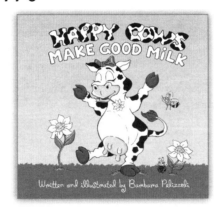

Marvin Sees the World

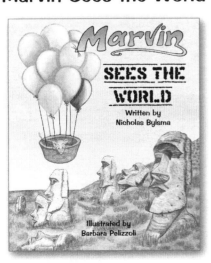

The Moon

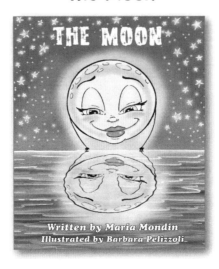

Be Proud of Yourself

COLORING BOOKS

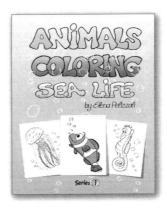

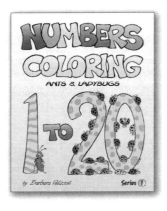

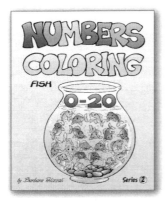

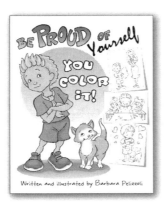

JOURNALS & NOTEBOOKS

Made in the USA
Middletown, DE
16 February 2016